Cat
Lady

Robyn L Stacey

DEDICATION

To all the past saints, recognized and unrecognized,
who dedicated their lives to making animals' lives better.
To all the present saints, recognized and unrecognized,
who dedicate their lives to making animals' lives better.
To all the future saints, recognized and unrecognized,
who will dedicate their lives to making animals' lives better.

God has bestowed on us
Warm fuzzy gifts from above;
Pets of all sizes and shapes –
Four-legged bundles of love.
excerpt from the poem
Blessings from Above written by Robyn L Stacey

To all the critters who have been blessings to me and my
family from Above. I love all y'all, now and forever.

CONTENTS

ACKNOWLEDGMENTS

Special thanks to God for His love, blessings and mercy.

Thank you, God, for all the cats, dogs, rabbits, etc. you have bestowed on me to care for and share this life with.

Thank you, God, for the inspiration for this story and your guidance during the writing process.

Special thanks to Grant and Lisa Stanford.

A Gathering Of Cats

Mysterious. Regal. From a lofty perch, we watch. Haunting eyes pierce the darkness. We stealthily hunt our prey. Mesmerized by shiny objects and anything that moves. Good natured little buddies always ready for play. Throughout the ages, cats have been loved and loathed, worshipped and feared.

I, personally, enjoy being loved and worshipped.

Who am I? Oh, I'm Trudy. Little brown tabby cat. I was found as a young kitten in a clearing meowing in a panic. I got myself lost from my mama. I was following her when I looked down at a little black cricket crawling in front of me. When I looked up, mama was gone. I cried out for her over and over, but I guess she didn't hear me. A human, a kind gentleman, heard my mews and scooped me up. It was a chilly night. He placed me inside his jacket and took me in his house. I was given some food and a warm place to sleep. I thought to myself: *This is nice. I think I'll stick around a while,* and I did.

Recently, I went to the Saint Francis of Assisi pet blessing at church. Who's Saint Francis of Assisi? He's the patron saint of animals. He watches over us, but he's not the only one. God loves us so much He has given us several saints who have taken His command to heart. In Genesis 1:26, God said: *Let us make man to*

our image and likeness: and let him have dominion over the fishes of the sea, and the fowls of the air, and the beasts, and the whole earth, and every creeping creature that moveth upon the earth. Even today, there are so many humans that dedicate their lives to caring for us animals. Some of those great caretakers take us to church every year to get a special blessing of God. Well, this year, some of us got together at church and listened to the story of the original cat lady.

I met up with several friends of mine, and I made a few more.

I saw Lolita approaching the line for the pet blessing. She's a pretty black and white kitty I've known for some time. "Hi, Lolita!" I exclaimed.

"Hi, Trudy," Lolita meowed back. "Wow! Look at all the dogs here, Trudy."

This was Lolita's first pet blessing; so, I explained, "Yeah, I know. Even though Saint Francis of Assisi is the patron of all animals, humans tend to focus on bringing their dogs to the annual blessing."

Lolita marveled at all the dogs. Big and small. Some tall and thin. Others short and wide. While we were watching the dogs, some of our friends walked up.

"Hey, Trudy and Lolita, do you ever wonder if there's a patron saint just for us cats?" Ranger asked walking up with Trinity and Dino Martino.

Ranger's a silver tabby I met here last year. Dino, a silver, tan and white tabby, is Ranger's best bud. Trinity is a black and white with a black boop button on the top of his white nose. I think he's kind of cute. What's a boop button? Well, sometimes humans like to touch our noses just at the top and say "boop."

Trinity has his spot specially marked; so, we call it the boop button.

"Sure, Ranger," I replied. "She's the original cat lady."

"How do you know our patron saint is a girl?" Dino asked.

"Because I'm named for her," I sarcastically retorted, as I stood, arched my back slightly, straightened my tail pointing it high to the sky and strutted around Dino.

"Watch out, Dino, she's a spitfire!" Trinity warned cocking his head.

Dino rolled his eyes upward.

With a slightly suspicious tone, Ranger queried, "soooo, there's a Saint Trudy?"

"Weeeeeell," I pawed in the dirt, "her name is Gertrude."

"Trudy is short for Gertrude." Lolita quickly came to my defense.

Trinity, nose high in the air, slightly distracted by a ladybug, asked, "Do you know anything else about her?"

"Not really, but I know who does." I said sitting back down.

"Who?" Lolita asked.

"Teddy." I answered.

Ranger scanned the area, "You mean the old man?"

"Yep!"

Teddy's well known amongst us cats. A handsome blue Siamese. Blue means he's gray. He has the most gorgeous blue eyes. He's been around forever. He's 18 years old in human years. That's got to be a hundred in cat years.

"He's so old he probably knew her," Jake snickered while rubbing back and forth against his dog friend, Shasta.

A large white male with gray spots and a gray tail with big round chartreuse colored eyes, Jake looks like he got mistaken for the donkey at a child's party while they were playing pin the tail on the donkey.

Katy and Amber walked up behind Jake.

Katy, a shy black and white tuxedo cat, always has a smile on. OK, well, she doesn't have a choice. Her white markings make her look like

she's smiling all the time. Amber, like Teddy, is one of the oldest cats I know. She's a peach colored $17\frac{1}{2}$ year old tabby. She's lucky to be here. She was hit by a car when she was about 6 months old. Some nice humans stopped and picked her up off the side of the road and brought her to a veterinarian. She's been tailless since the accident.

"That's not very nice!" Amber snapped. Her ears drawn back and whiskers bristled forward.

"Feeling sympathetic, Amber?" Jake teased back.

Amber glared at Jake.

"Did Teddy come today?" Katy asked before Amber could hiss at Jake.

Everyone looked at each other and shrugged.

"Is that him?" Dino motioned with his nose in Teddy's direction.

We all turned to look. The sun glistened off his old blue eyes which he held at a squint to ward off the glare of the sun. He gently laid his old body down in a sunny spot in the soft grass closing his tired eyes.

"Do you think we should ask him?" Lolita whispered.

"Why not?" I asked parading across the grass, head held high and tail straight up with just a slight hook at the end pointing in the direction I was headed.

The other cats soon followed me in pursuit of Teddy. We walked through several groups of dogs. Some ignored us. Some just leered at us.

Some made us a little nervous not knowing if they would take up chase. Thank you, God, for leashes!

"Teddy." Amber quietly called out.

Teddy was half sitting as if it would hurt to finish lying down, eyes closed, basking in the sun. He slowly opened his tired eyes to see us all before him.

"What's up, y'all?" Teddy asked.

"Trudy here says you know all about Saint Gertrude, the patroness of cats!" Lolita blurted out in excitement.

"Yep, I know about her." Teddy replied.

"Can you tell *us* about her?" Trinity asked.

"I suppose I can. Y'all have a seat."

As Teddy began the story of Saint Gertrude, other cats started to gather around. Dev, another elderly long-haired FIV positive red tabby, sat nearby nodding his head in approval of all Teddy said. He, too, knew the story. Dev's son and daughter, Dusty and Sandy, were there. Sisters, Bonnie and Krissy, who brought her three sons and daughter - Colt, Dakota, Kimber and Daisy - were there. Ranger's sister, Annie, followed her brother. Brothers, Rio Bravo and Tony, came with a silver Siamese tabby, Capri. Heather, whose mother was from another litter of Krissy's, stopped by to listen. Abilene, Aubrey, Kirby, Tioga, Tyler, Sierra, Hondo, Laredo, Penny and Rikki also made an appearance. Some feral cats from the area joined in, as well, but kept their distance: Sylvia, Eli, Lira, Nikki, Princess, Meezer, Bunny and a couple of tabbies, Tab and Hunter.

I suppose we must've made quite the scene! A collection of cats of all sorts gathered around one storytelling Siamese.

FINDING ROSIE

Teddy began to recall the story of Saint Gertrude:

Long before Saint Francis of Assisi preached to the birds and brokered peace between Brother Wolf and the town of Gubbio, Italy, Gertrude was caring for the cats of Nivelles.

A little background, I suppose, would be a good start. The year was 626 when Gertrude was born in Landen, Belgium. Her father, Pepin, moved his family to Nivelles. Nivelles was a village of about forty-eight square miles in central Belgium. The village was rebuilt by Pepin, who was also known as Pippen the Elder. Pepin and his wife, Itta of Metz, had several children including sons, Grimoald and Bavo, and daughters, Begga and Gertrude.

Pepin was an influential, wealthy man in the region. When King Clothar II reached the end of his reign, Pepin persuaded him to crown Dagobert, Clothar's son, as king of Austrasia.

With Dagobert following his father to the throne, Pepin was appointed mayor of the palace. He moved his family within the king's court.

Pepin and Itta's children married into families of wealth, power and political connections. When Gertrude was about ten years old, her father hosted a banquet in her honor. The king, who attended the banquet, asked Gertrude if she'd like to marry the duke of the Austrasians. Young Gertrude declined the offer saying she would have no earthly spouse. She, instead, had already decided to dedicate her life to the Lord, Jesus Christ.

Gertrude was a good child. Obedient and studious. She always tried to help family, friends and strangers... and cats. She loved to tend to the gardens in the king's court. She loved the colors, the textures, the aromas. She was in awe of God's creations. She would spend hours in both the flower and vegetable gardens oftentimes in prayer. Gertrude felt closer to God here.

While in the gardens, nearby the elegant pink rose bush, the garden centerpiece, kneeling in prayer, she heard a sound.

Mew

Gertrude tried to concentrate on her prayers, but the little sound once again interrupted her.

Mew

Gertrude felt a warm, soft, cottony body rub against her and then curl up into a ball at her knees. No longer able to concentrate on her prayers, she looked down. Her eyes were met by the wide eyes of a little brown tabby and white kitten.

Mew

Gertrude smiled and mimicked the sound the kitten made.

The kitten sat up and pawed at Gertrude, *mee-yew.*

Gertrude gently lifted the kitten, cradling it in her arms, "where did you come from?"

The little kitten snuggled into Gertrude's arms and chest and began to purr.

Gertrude smiled and looked at the kitten. She wondered what to call the little fuzz ball. She glanced up to see the sun's rays shining through the pastel flowers adorning the rose bush before her.

"Rose!" Gertrude exclaimed. "Your name shall be Rose, and I'll call you Rosie."

In the following days and months, the little kitten grew into a beautiful cat. Gertrude and Rosie became constant companions. Rosie liked to chase butterflies in the garden showing her acrobatic grace. Gertrude watched with a smile on her face. Oftentimes, Gertrude sat beneath the shade of a large tree reading the Holy Scriptures. Rosie took advantage of these peaceful moments and curled up in Gertrude's lap.

Gertrude was about 13 or 14 when her father, Pepin, died, about 639 or 640. Pepin was a good man. A man of God. Gertrude knew her father was in God's favor when he died, but still, she missed her dad. She missed his love. She missed the way he'd smile at the good works she did. She missed his words of encouragement. She missed his gentle arms and reassuring hands that hugged her and made her feel safe.

In the days following his death, Gertrude caught herself gazing at the chair where her dad sat.

Prrrrrrrt. Rosie gently rubbed against her, weaving in and out of her legs.

Gertrude looked down at her furry little friend and smiled. "You miss him, too, don't you, Rosie?"

Mrow

Gertrude bent down and picked up Rosie. She held her close, buried her face in Rosie's fur and gently petted her side. Rosie rubbed her nose against Gertrude's chin. As a tear fell from her eye, she felt the roughness of Rosie's tongue like grit against her cheek.

Rosie, like the Holy Scriptures, was a great comfort to Gertrude during her time of grief. The blessing of the little cat who comforted her reminded Gertrude of the Matthew 5:4 verse *Blessed are they that mourn for they shall be comforted.* Some would ask: where was God? Where is He to comfort as promised? Gertrude knew. She knew God used little Rosie to grant this blessing, for Rosie was a creation of God and God lives in her.

Following the death of her husband, Itta, too, grieved, but her ability to grieve was short lived. A land-holding widow in the seventh century needed to protect her family and wealth. Marriage was one way to gain land, become wealthy and powerful. Gertrude had many suitors who sought her hand in marriage, as well as the family's land and riches. Gertrude, however, refused them all. Her life belonged to her Lord. Itta began construction of an abbey. Some believe, due to these seventh century beliefs, Itta constructed the abbey as protection for her and her daughter. Others believe the bishop of Maastricht, later to become Saint Amand, urged Itta to build the abbey. Bishop Amand preached at Itta's home. It is believed he asked her to build the abbey when he was at the home preaching. Whatever Itta's reasons for building the abbey, she used some of her husband's land and funds to build the double monastery at Nivelles.

Because of Gertrude's youth, Itta became the abbey's first abbess. Itta's intent was for Gertrude to be the abbess; therefore, she prepared Gertrude for the position. As Itta lay ill, she believed Gertrude, at the age of twenty years, was old enough to assume the role of abbess of the Nivelles abbey. Gertrude had proven herself a handmaid of the Lord. She was a mystic, gifted with visions. She was bright, kind and mature beyond her years. A charitable young woman who devoted herself to the sick, elderly and poor. Gertrude had memorized much of the Holy Scriptures and passages from books on divine law. She explained the hidden mysteries of parables to those who'd listen.

Itta bestowed the role of abbess on Gertrude. Being in favor with God, Itta quietly joined her husband in eternal sleep. Once again, Rosie comforted Gertrude.

GERTRUDE & ROSIE RESCUE LUCY

Gertrude spent the early morning hours in the monastery garden. It was where she found solace and felt close to God. The garden grew with Gertrude's desire to feed people. With Rosie by her side, she picked vegetables to give to the poor and elderly of Nivelles. Word spread of her garden. People came from far and wide to taste the fruits of her labor as well as gain the fruits of the Holy Spirit. Outside the walls of the monastery, Gertrude offered fruits and vegetables from the garden with a warm smile and words of wisdom from the Scriptures. She sent travelers on their way with blessings from Scripture such as Psalm 145:9 (ESV) and 2 Corinthians

13:14: *The Lord is good to all and His Mercy is over all that He has made. May the grace of our Lord Jesus Christ, and the charity of God, and the communication of the Holy Ghost be with you.*

One early morning, Gertrude and Rosie were walking through the garden. Rosie left Gertrude's side. Between the rows of leafy vegetables, Rosie's tail, high and curled slightly

at the tip pointing in the direction she moved, was all Gertrude could see. Rosie cautiously approached a corner of the garden where a small shed stood. Her whiskers stood straight forward, twitching. Gertrude watched curiously. When Rosie didn't return in a short time, Gertrude headed to the shed. The shed contained some gardening tools and seeds Gertrude used in the garden. As she drew closer, she could hear tiny mews. Where were they coming from? In the shed? Under the shed? Behind the shed?

Rosie heard Gertrude draw near. She poked her head out from the side of the shed. The small cat stood between the outer wall surrounding the monastery and the little shed.

Mrow

"What's there, Rosie?"

Rosie held her head high and her whiskers forward. Her eyes were wide and alert, glistening in the sun. Her ears rotated back and forth listening to Gertrude and her find beside the shed.

"Is something back there?"

Rosie abruptly turned, tail arched high above her back and walked back between the wall and the shed.

"Let's have a look, then."

Gertrude followed Rosie's lead. There, lying between the shed and the wall, was a black mama cat with her kittens. Gertrude had barely enough room to get to them. Surprised the cat didn't attempt to run, Gertrude gently petted the mama cat. The mama cat purred. Rosie looked on.

"What do you think, Rosie?"

Mrow

"You're right. We should bring them inside."

Gertrude gently picked up each kitten. The mama cat sat and watched closely. There were three. She placed them in the bucket she had brought for the vegetables. With her kittens safe in the bucket, the mama cat got up and followed Gertrude and Rosie back to the monastery.

Once inside, Gertrude placed some bedding in an old wooden firewood box. She placed the kittens one by one in the box. The mama cat went into the box and began to nurse the kittens. Gertrude offered the mama cat some scrap food from Rosie's scrap jar. Gertrude supplemented Rosie's meals of mice and insects with leftover scraps from the kitchen.

Silently, with an internal smile, Rosie sat and watched. She was proud she rescued the mama and her kittens.

Satisfied the mama cat and her kittens were settled into their box, Gertrude left to finish her day's work of tending the gardens, delivering food to the poor and elderly and checking on some travelers who had stayed the night at the abbey.

When night fell, Gertrude went back to her room. Rosie, always by Gertrude's side, confidently weaved back and forth in front of Gertrude.

"Rosie, you're going to trip me. Silly girl!"

Prrrrrtttt. Rosie rubbed against Gertrude, strutted with her tail high above her back and occasionally glanced back at Gertrude.

Gertrude smiled back at the little tabby and white cat.

Before turning into bed, Gertrude said her nightly prayers and checked on the mama cat and her kittens.

"What's your name, mama?" Gertrude quietly asked the mama cat.

"Lucy," she responded.

©2018 Paws4Critters Designs

©2018 Paws4Critters Designs

Gertrude sat back. She looked over at Rosie. Rosie tilted her head slightly to the left and then to the right. Gertrude returned her gaze to Lucy.

"Lucy." Gertrude repeated. "Well, Lucy, how is it you can talk to me?"

"It's not that *I* can talk to *you*, Gertrude. It's that *you* can understand *me*."

"Blessed be God!"

For a moment, Gertrude just stared at Lucy and her kittens trying to make sense of it.

"*I* can understand *you*? No one else here can hear you?"

"Oh, they can hear me. They just don't hear me the way you do."

"How is it that I can understand you and others can not?"

"God has found favor with you and bestowed gifts on you."

Gertrude smiled. She petted Lucy, and Lucy arched her back into Gertrude's hand.

Gertrude left Lucy and the kittens for the night. She readied for bed and tucked herself in. Rosie curled up beside her after giving herself a bath.

FRISCO'S STAR

Gertrude awoke feeling watched. She opened her eyes. Lucy, whiskers forward, ears perked, sat wide-eyed staring at Gertrude. Gertrude rose up and rested on her elbow.

"What's the matter, Lucy?"

"Why did God choose you? God has given humans all this..." Lucy rotated her head looking about the room and finally gazing out the little window across the room where the gardens could be seen. "Does God care about us? Does God care about cats... about any of the animals of this world?"

"Of course He does, Lucy. Before God made

humans, he made all the animals of the earth. God said: *Let the earth bring forth the living creature in its kind, cattle and creeping things, and beasts of the earth, according to their kinds. And it was so done. And God made the beasts of the earth according to their kinds, and cattle, and every thing that creepeth on the earth after its kind. And God saw that it was good.* Have you not heard the story of Noah?"

"No." Lucy quietly whispered, folding her ears back against her head and lowering her head, slightly.

"Noah was chosen by God to save all the animals of the earth when God was angry with humans. Humans let Him down. They would not abide by God's laws. It made God very angry, and He decided to punish them by flooding the earth. God knew, though, the animals did not wrong Him. He instructed Noah, a good, devout man, to gather all the animals of the earth, male and female, onto an ark. God then flooded the earth with continuous rain for forty days and forty nights. God did not forget about the cat. Both male and female survived the flood aboard the ark."

Rosie joined Lucy sitting on the bed before Gertrude.

Gertrude continued, "Even at the birth of Jesus, our Lord and Savior, a cat was present. Jesus was born in a stable of sorts. Among those who first laid eyes on Him were cattle, a donkey, sheep from the shepherds' fields and a little tabby cat name Lily whose job it was to keep the mice out of the cattle trough. When little Jesus was in the manger, Lily, who had been a mother herself, took it upon herself to keep the baby Jesus warm by curling up with

him. His mother, Mary, was ever so grateful to the little cat. It is said, when she petted Lily, her gratitude became emblazoned across the tabby's forehead marking her and all like her for eternity with Mary's initial "M."

Both cats sat, statuesque, wide-eyed and mesmerized by what Gertrude related to them. Soon, though, Lucy once again dropped her head and lowered her ears. Her eyes lost their sparkle.

Gertrude noticed the change in Lucy, "Why do you ask such a thing?" Gertrude gently lifted Lucy's chin to look into her emerald eyes.

"One of my kittens is ill. He's not going to make it. Why would God give me this little one only to take him away?"

Lucy focused her ears forward waiting for a response.

"Well, Lucy, sometimes, God bestows on us little blessings from above for us to love and hold for just a little while. He chooses the most precious gifts from His beautiful garden, He lends them to us to care for, to love, faithfully, unconditionally, to the very end. He touches our hearts with the souls of others; so, that we might know *His* love. Although He may take them from us after many years or only a few days, He has granted us a special blessing to cherish for all our lives. Our blessing from above will soon fade into a memory, but we will never be the same. The blessing will always be with us. Our hearts will be bigger. We will think of the love and smile. Our lives will have been fuller because of the blessing of love God has bestowed on us. Remember this, He could have given that blessing to anyone, but He chose *you*. He chose you to care for something – *someone* – very special to *Him*. He thought so highly of *you* He entrusted *you* to care for and love His wonderful gift."

Lucy stood, jumped off the bed and calmly walked back to her box of kittens. Rosie and Gertrude followed. It was still in the early morning hours. The sun had not yet risen. Gertrude sat on the floor with Rosie and watched as Lucy gently cleaned her sick kitten.

"What's his name, Lucy?" Rosie asked.

"Frisco."

"That's a wonderful name," Gertrude smiled.

"What will become of him, Gertrude?" Lucy asked looking up for reassurance.

"Remember how Noah took all the animals on the ark?"

"Yes."

"God made a promise to all. He promised to never flood the earth again. His promise was a rainbow. To this day, after it rains, the rainbow appears as a reminder of a promise long ago. The promise may be a pact with humans, but God did not abandon his creatures. On the other side of the rainbow is a luscious green pasture of beautifully scented flowers, large shade trees, butterflies to chase and ponds to play in. When their earthly life has come to an end, God sends an angel to carry those pets over the rainbow where they will wait to be reunited with their caretakers."

"It sounds wonderful," Rosie whispered.

"Yes, it does, but what about those who have no human caretaker? I belong to no one. My kittens are but mine alone. What becomes of us?" Lucy solemnly pondered.

"Lucy, do you ever look up at the night sky? All the twinkling stars gazing back down at you. Does it make you feel small and insignificant? Don't let it. They are proof no matter how small you are *you* are never insignificant in the eyes of God. He made you. He knew you before you were born. For God said, *"before I formed you in the womb I knew you, before you were born I set you apart."* (NAS) You, too, are a gift from God. He created you, and you are special to Him. God maintains a special gift for all those who have no human caretakers. He sends an angel to them as well, but they are brought before *Him*. He tends to them personally giving them the gift of lighting the way for all those who are lost in the night. You are the twinkle in His eye, Lucy. You will never be forgotten. Your kitten will never be forgotten. When we look up into the night sky, there you will be."

Comforted by Gertrude's words, Lucy pawed her sick kitten closer to her and lovingly caressed the baby with her tongue. As she did so, Frisco drew his final breath. Gertrude wiped her eyes. She knew the mama cat was hurting. She, too, felt the loss. The silence was deafening.

Gertrude looked up when she heard Rosie gasp. The room was filled with light, but the sun was still another hour before its ascent. Gertrude

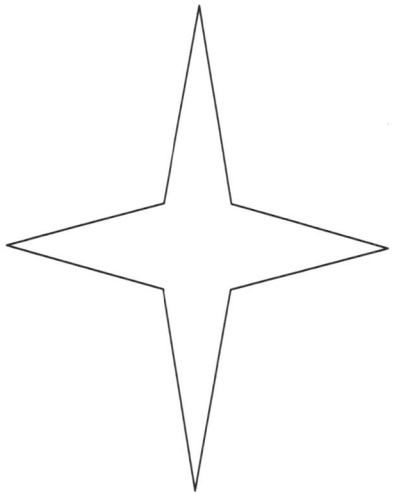

rose up and went to the window. There high in the early morning sky was a bright star shining down lighting the entire room.

"There. You see that, Lucy?" Gertrude asked pointing to the shining star. "*That's* your little boy, Frisco."

Lucy snuggled Frisco's lifeless body one last time.

When the sun rose, Lucy and Rosie

accompanied Gertrude to the garden where
the rose bush stood front and center.
Gertrude buried little Frisco in the shadows of
the rose bush.

Heidi Rescues Cadon

When the kittens were old enough, Lucy and her two remaining kittens accompanied Rosie and Gertrude in the garden and in a rare excursion outside the monastery walls delivering fruits and vegetables to the townsfolk of Nivelles, as well as any travelers they met.

They came upon a boy sitting on a dirt path playing with some stones. Gertrude watched the young boy stack the stones and then knock them down with a stick. Tears streamed down the boy's face.

"What's the matter?" Gertrude asked.

The little boy didn't respond. He never even looked up. He continued to restack the stones and knock them down again.

Seeing Gertrude wasn't getting a response from the boy, Rosie walked up to him. She got just close enough to position her tail so it would

brush against his face just under his nose. The boy wiped at his face to remove the tail hairs from his nose. Rosie turned and walked back, repeating her act. Again, the boy wiped at his face. Rosie, then, sat directly in front of the boy between him and his stack of rocks.

Forced to confront the cat, the little boy looked at Rosie. He frowned.

Mrow Rosie stood up, leaned forward and touched her nose to the boy's.

He rubbed the wetness from his nose.

Finally, the boy looked up at Gertrude; then, down at Rosie. He wiped his eyes, but said nothing. Rosie got closer and sat with her paws in the child's lap. She pushed her head into his tiny hand forcing him to pet her. When he placed his hand on her, she stood and walked, arching her back and holding her tail upright. He smiled as he petted the little tabby and white cat from head to tail.

Gertrude sat down beside him. Lucy and her kittens joined Rosie in rubbing on the boy and forcing him to pet them.

Prrrrrt Lucy purred as she was petted.

"They're soft," the boy finally spoke.

"Yes, they are." Gertrude answered.

"Do they have names?"

"This is Rosie… and Lucy. The white male kitten with the spots is Valentine. The female tabby is Heidi." Gertrude pointed to each cat.

"Why do you have them?" the boy asked.

"God has given them to me for company. They are like family." Gertrude responded.

"I don't have any family."

"No family? Where's your mom and dad?"

"They got sick and went to heaven."

"I see."

Heidi crawled up into the little boy's lap. He petted her and she responded by licking and nibbling his hand.

"What's your name?" Gertrude asked.

"Cadon," the boy responded.

"Cadon, do you live around here?"

He shook his head in agreement.

"Where do you live?" Gertrude pressed.

"With my aunt and uncle down the road," he said as he pointed.

"Do you like the kitty?"

"Yes!" Cadon smiled as he lifted the kitten under her front paws up to his face.

Heidi hung there until Cadon pulled her close to his body and hugged her.

Mmeh Heidi squeaked as the boy hugged her tight.

"Can I have her?" Cadon asked.

"If it's ok with your aunt and uncle," Gertrude said firmly.

Gertrude remembered how Rosie helped her through the loss of her father and then her mother. She knew Heidi would be a great comfort to Cadon. She also knew she'd have to get his aunt and uncle's approval.

Photo courtesy of Grant and Lisa Stanford

"Come, let's go talk to your aunt and uncle about Heidi." Gertrude said standing.

She clasped the boy's hand in hers and started down the road in the direction he pointed. Cadon held tightly onto Heidi. Heidi clung tightly to Cadon. Rosie, Lucy and Valentine led the way with Valentine between Rosie and Lucy. All three cats walked proudly with their tails high and their whiskers forward catching the slight breeze.

As they crossed a small, bridge-covered creek, a woman stood in the doorway of a small cottage. Her hands on her hips. As they drew closer, Gertrude worried the boy was in trouble. Gertrude smiled at the woman as they approached.

"Where have you been? You had us worried sick!" the woman exclaimed.

"He was on the other side of the creek. Can we talk?" Gertrude asked the woman in a quiet humble tone.

"Yes. Please do come in," the aunt invited showing Gertrude the open door.

"My name is Gertrude."

"Good to meet you. My name is Lisa."

The women went inside while Cadon stayed outside with the cats. Gertrude explained to Lisa how she came upon Cadon. She told her he was missing his parents. Lisa told Gertrude it hadn't been long since they passed, and he was having a difficult time.

"When my parents died, Rosie was there for me. She was my constant companion. She helped me through a difficult time. When I was down and sad, she was there to offer her friendship and brought a smile to my face. She gave me a reason to be alive. When I thought she depended on me for her care, I found I also depended on her. She is a blessing from God. Through her, God shows me He cares."

"Do you think that kitten can do the same for Cadon?" Lisa asked watching Cadon with Heidi through the window.

"Yes, I do." Gertrude responded with a smile.

"Would it be ok for him to keep her?"

Gertrude joined Lisa at the window, "It appears to be God's will."

Lisa went to the door and called to Cadon to

come in. Cadon, still holding Heidi tight in his arms, entered the house followed by Lucy, Rosie and Valentine.

"Can I keep her?" Cadon asked sitting down in a chair with Heidi.

Photo courtesy of Grant and Lisa Stanford

"Yes, you can keep her," Lisa told him.

Cadon turned to Gertrude and smiled a wide smile, "thank you!"

Photo courtesy of Grant and Lisa Stanford

Lisa invited Gertrude to stay for dinner. Gertrude, seeing the family was poor and had little to offer, told Lisa she appreciated the invitation, but she couldn't impose. Gertrude gave Lisa the basket of vegetables she was carrying instead, and told her she'd be back to check on them from time to time.

Gertrude, Rosie, Lucy and Valentine left and headed back to the monastery.

The Original Cat Lady

Since rescuing Lucy and her kittens, cats from all around the Nivelles area sought Gertrude's help and guidance. She helped mother cats find homes for their kittens, and then, found homes for them as well.

Gertrude's hospitality was well known as she would often take in travelers, pilgrims, widows and orphans. The people of Nivelles came to her when they needed a little extra help. Gertrude was always welcoming and offered Scripture teachings as well as a place to eat and sleep. She brought the cats and kittens with her when she tended to those who sought refuge at the monastery.

Gertrude told the villagers the cats could help them in ridding their homes, farms and pastures of rodents and insects. She explained her gardens were nearly free from vermin and the dreaded locust. The monastery animals - goats, pigs, cow and calf - ate from clean troughs. Gertrude told them some of the cats stayed outside in the outbuildings with the other animals, and some stayed in the monastery keeping it free from pests. The people listened and were amazed at Gertrude's claims.

Farmers, shepherds, housewives and children took in Gertrude's cats and kittens. The cats taught the kittens to hunt their quarry. The kittens grew into great hunters serving their masters and mistresses well. The village of Nivelles reaped the benefits of Gertrude's cats. Travelers came from other areas of Belgium and beyond in search of the little cat monastery where Gertrude saved and found homes for wayward cats and kittens. The children loved to play with the kittens and cuddle with the cats.

Her work with the poor, elderly, widows and

orphans, and even travelers, did not rattle anyone. Eventually, as is with all things, some were not keen on her helping the little furry beasts. Gertrude had many inquiring why she wasted her time on these hideous beasts that prowled around in the dark of night. They warned her any creature that lived for the night could not be of God. They told her these beasts were evil and their poor condition was a curse from God for their evil ways. God couldn't possibly want her to nurse these wicked creatures back to health and trick unsuspecting villagers into adopting them. Gertrude was accused of placing evil in the homes of good Christians. Some feared taking in these creatures would bring the wrath of God upon their house.

Gertrude stood her ground. She challenged her critics. She questioned their allegiances to God. Gertrude quoted Scripture verse after Scripture verse:

"In Matthew 6:26, the birds of the air are provided for by our heavenly Father, but what if one falls to the earth in front of you. Do you let it lie or do you tend to it? What if our

Lord is testing your charity? Matthew 7:12 (JB) tells us: *always treat others as you would like them to treat you; that is the Law and the Prophets.* One could say this pertains only to humans, but how you treat your fellow man may be judged by how you treat all God's creations. If you walk on by the lowliest creature in need, who's to say you will not walk on by one of your own in need.

Remember Jesus' teaching: *A certain man went down from Jerusalem to Jericho, and fell among robbers, who also stripped him, and having wounded him went away, leaving him half dead. And it chanced, that a certain priest went down the same way: and seeing him, passed by. In like manner also a Levite, when he was near the place and saw him, passed by. But a certain Samaritan being on his journey, came near him; and seeing him, was moved with compassion. And going up to him, bound up his wounds, pouring in oil and wine: and setting him upon his own beast, brought him to an inn, and took care of him. And the next day he took out two pence, and gave to the host, and said: Take care of him; and whatsoever thou shalt spend over and above, I, at my return, will repay thee. Which of these three, in thy opinion, was neighbor to him that fell among the robbers? But he said: He that showed mercy to him. And Jesus said to him: Go, and do thou in like manner.*

Again, those who will walk on by the creature in need, which God has made, will, then, also walk on by the man, woman or child who is in need.

Do you also tend to your flocks, human or

animal? Then, why should you not care for *all* of God's creatures? It is told in Isaiah 40:11 *He shall feed His flock like a shepherd: He shall gather together the lambs with His arm, and shall take them up in his bosom, and He Himself shall carry them that are with young.* Jesus, himself, stated in Luke 15:4-5, "*What man of you that hath an hundred sheep: and if he shall lose one of them, doth he not leave the ninety-nine in the desert, and go after that which was lost, until he find it? And when he hath found it, lay it upon his shoulders, rejoicing.*" True, Jesus used this parable to tell of how God will always be there for man, even if he strays and sins. His mercy is always with us; yet, you would condemn one of God's creatures because you do not understand its place in this world? How do you reconcile this with our Lord?

Let everything that has breath praise the Lord. Psalm 150:6 (NAS) explicitly tells us even cats worship the Lord.

Ecclesiastes 12:7 (JB) instructs us *the dust returns to the earth from which it came, and the spirit returns to God who gave it.* On the sixth day, God created all the creatures of the earth. They are His. God always reclaims what is His.

Recall in Luke 3:6 *all flesh shall see the Salvation of God.* He does not say except this one or except that one. If you have repented your sins and are in favor with God, our Lord will have mercy on you and you shall see the Salvation of God. *All* flesh. No exceptions."

This drew the attention of monks as far away as Ireland, including Foillan, with whom Gertrude became great friends. They visited her at the monastery many times. The Irish monasteries were widely known for their oral teachings. They often stopped by Nivelles on their way to Rome.

With the support of her friends and those who had adopted Gertrude's cats, many who questioned her soon saw the good in her work. They, too, found themselves adopting cats from Gertrude or caring for those they found on their journeys.

GERTRUDE'S LEGACY

Gertrude toiled from sunup to sundown tending
the monastery gardens, the poor, widows,
orphans, pilgrims and all who sought her help.
She seldom left the monastery. She rarely
took time for herself, but when she did, it was
in prayer alongside her cats. For Gertrude,
solace came in the Word of God and the furry
little felines that befriended her.

In the last years of her life, Gertrude
suffered illness. She had given so much of
herself. Her life of charity, fasting and
constant prayer took a toll on her.

Gertrude grew weak with exhaustion allowing

illness to set in. She continued with her daily routine as much as possible. Her cats knew something was wrong. They stayed by her side and watched over her by night.

Gertrude visited Rosie's grave one last time in the garden near the rose bush where Gertrude had found her as a kitten. Rosie had passed years ago after a happy, full life with Gertrude. Lucy, Valentine, who became a monastery barn cat, as well as little Frisco who died the night Gertrude and Rosie rescued them, were buried beside Rosie, having lived out their lives at the monastery. Although she loved all the monastery cats, Rosie was still her favorite. Rosie was that one special cat you meet once in a lifetime. She plucked a rose from the bush, as it already had begun to bloom, and laid it on Rosie's grave.

Gertrude prayed and kept vigils. She spoke with the Lord and asked for guidance. As time passed, she felt her life waning. During this difficult time, Gertrude accepted many visitors at the monastery. Many came to visit and offer their help.

In her last days, Gertrude passed her responsibilities of Abbess of Nivelles to her niece, Wulfetrud.

Ultan, another Irish monk and brother of Foillan, visited Gertrude while she was ill. Gertrude and Ultan spoke. He prophesied Gertrude would pass on the feast of Saint Patrick, which was the next day.

Gertrude spent her last hours in prayer and was given Holy Communion. On March 17, 659, Gertrude passed "joyously because blessed Bishop Patrick with the chosen angels of God were prepared to receive her,"[1] as Ultan had told her.

Her years were short, but her impact on

Nivelles and the lives of those around her, including her cats, would last for centuries. No one knows how many cats Gertrude rescued and cared for at the monastery, but rodents and insects were never a problem.

Teddy concluded the story with, "Gertrude was known to build churches, care for orphans, widows, captives and pilgrims. Her friends included traveling monks, other religious, especially the Irish... and cats!"

"So, Saint Gertrude was the original cat lady?" Ranger's sister, Annie, asked.

"Yes, I suppose, you could say that," Teddy answered.

"And I'm named for her!" Trudy exclaimed.

"She was also the first animal rescuer," Amber added.

"That was a great story, Teddy," said Penny, "I really enjoyed it."

"Thank God there are still folks like Saint Gertrude around," Krissy observed while looking at all the people that showed up for the St Francis of Assisi pet blessing.

"Yes, thank God!" Trudy and the other cats agreed.

REFERENCE

1. Vita Sanctae Geretrudis

About The Author

Robyn Stacey is an animal caretaker/rescuer, photographer, graphic designer, genealogist and writer. She inherited her love of animals from her mom and her interest in photography from her dad & maternal grandma. Robyn became interested in genealogy at the young age of at least 10 years old thanks to her dad's interest in the history of his father's family. Robyn is a proud United States Air Force brat and native Texan.

Quotes:
"My hope is for folks to see beyond the man-made world and, instead, see the beautiful world God has bestowed upon us!"
"Pawsing for Critters with Four Paws!"

Robyn's photography & Paws4Critters graphic design line can be purchased around the internet at:

robyn-stacey.pixels.com
www.robynstaceyphotos.etsy.com
www.cafepress.com/paws4critters
www.cafepress.com/americausa

and search "paws4critters" on Amazon.

Robyn has the following books published and available for purchase on Amazon.
Mama, Where Do Strays Go?
Brother Wolf The Wolf of Gubbio A Story of Saint Francis
Colorful Cats Adult Grayscale Coloring Book
Classic Cars Adult Grayscale Coloring Book
Orphaned By War The Stacy Saga

Follow Robyn's photography, graphic design and books on Facebook at
www.facebook.com/robynstaceypaws4crittersphotography
or her blog at http://paws4critters.blog

In remembrance of Saint Gertrude, please remember all the animals in your local shelters and rescues. They are always in need of volunteers. Donations of items such as food, training treats, blankets, printer paper, ink and services such as training, walking, etc. are things they need. Monetary donations of any size are always appreciated. Donations to local shelters and rescues are always better than national organizations that have employees to pay. Most local shelters and rescues are all volunteer; so, your donations go directly to helping to feed, house, vaccinate and spay/neuter rescued animals.

Thank you and God bless!

Made in the USA
Lexington, KY
07 December 2018